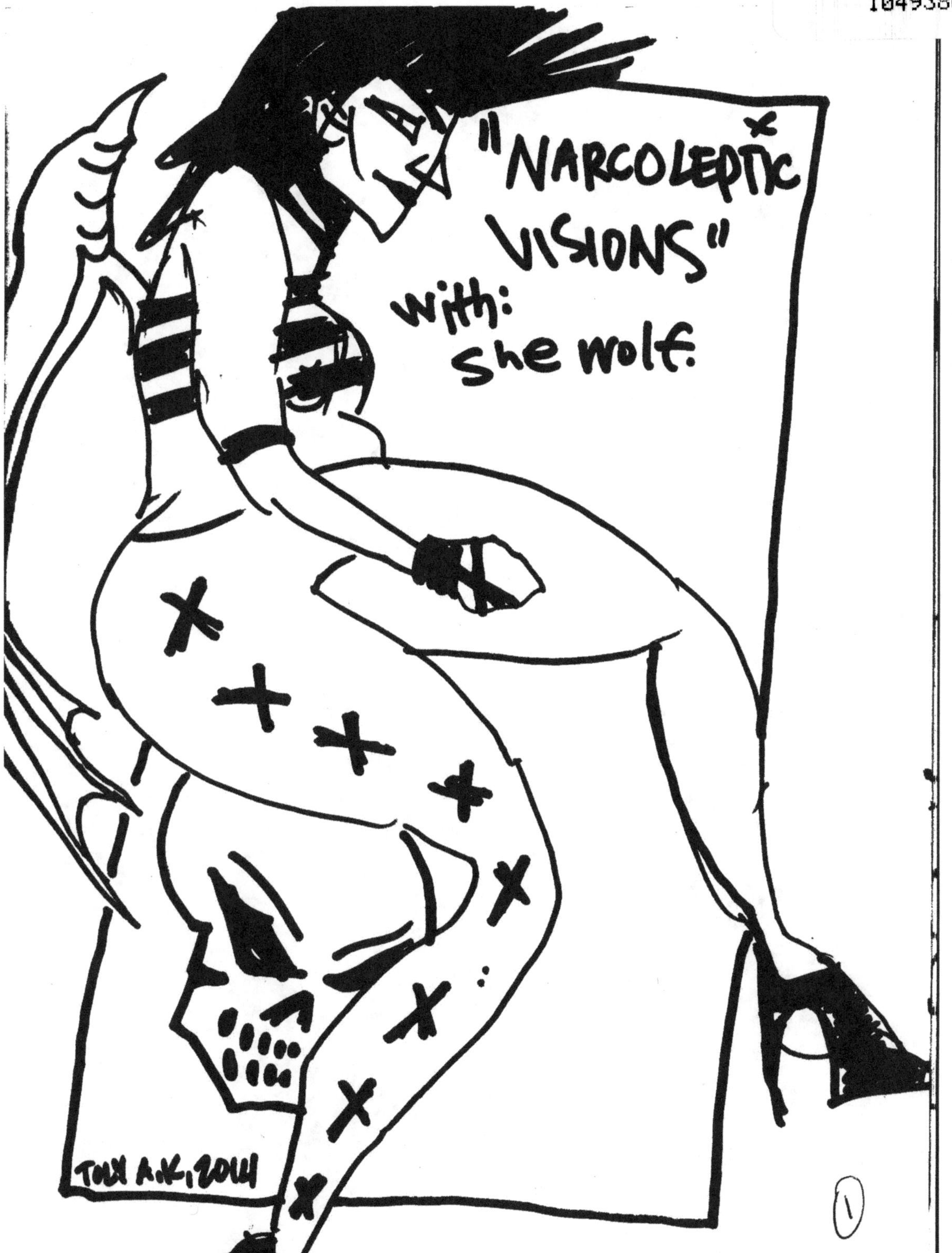

"NARCOLEPTIC VISIONS"

with: she wolf.

filtered on the lip of a lolly-pop ring, she stands dressed in black duct tape - straight edge and razor sharp. In a NIHILISTIC wet DREAM.

②

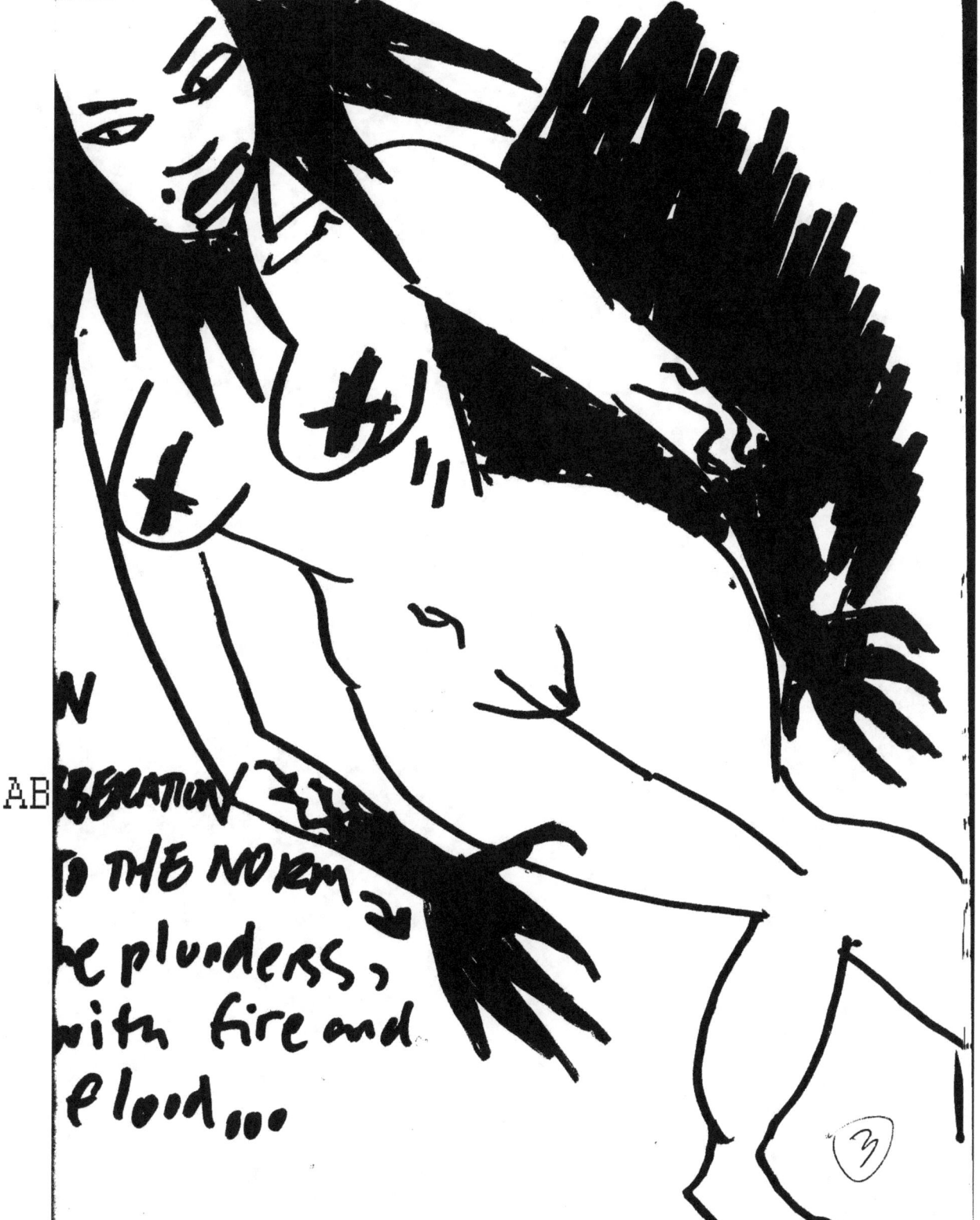

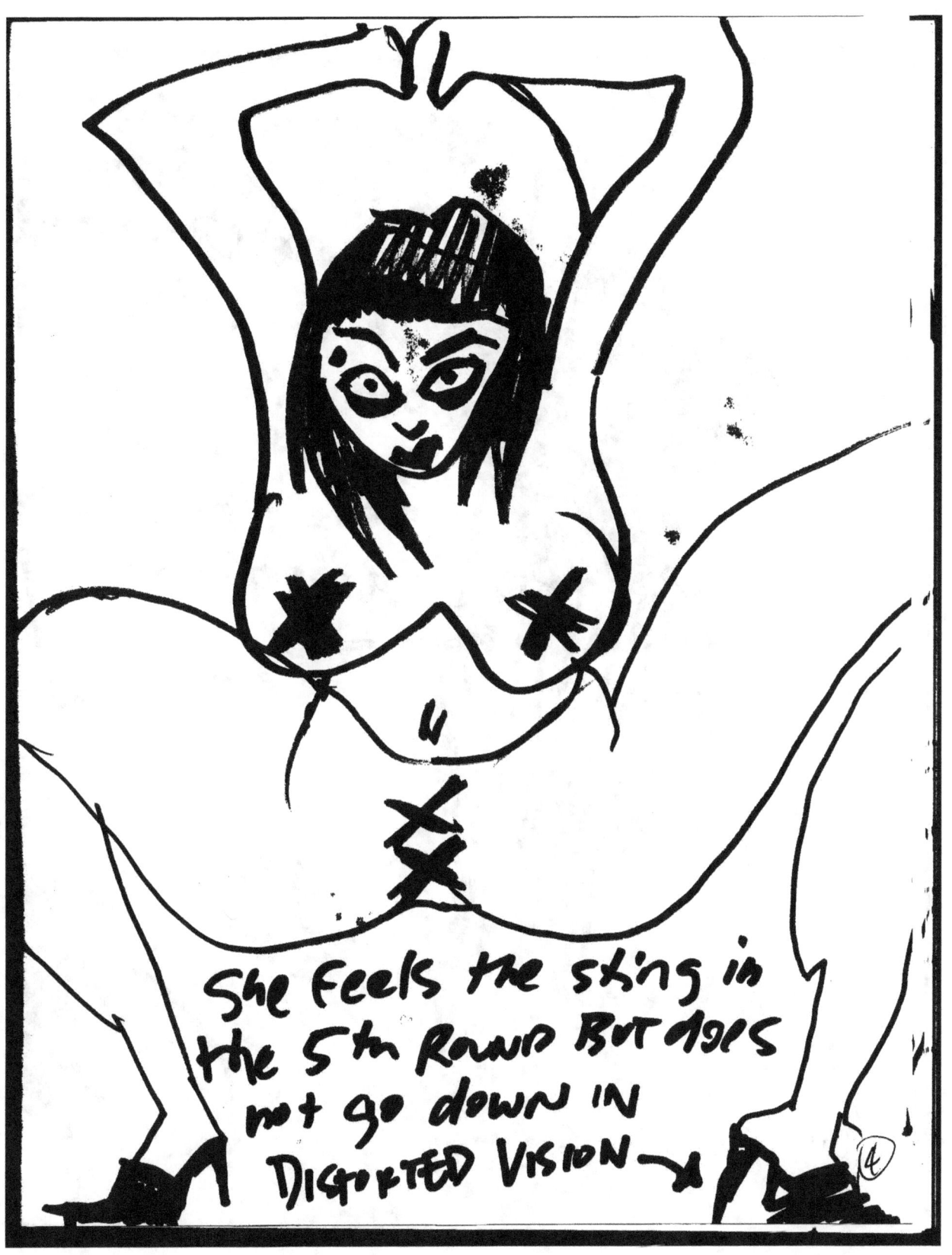

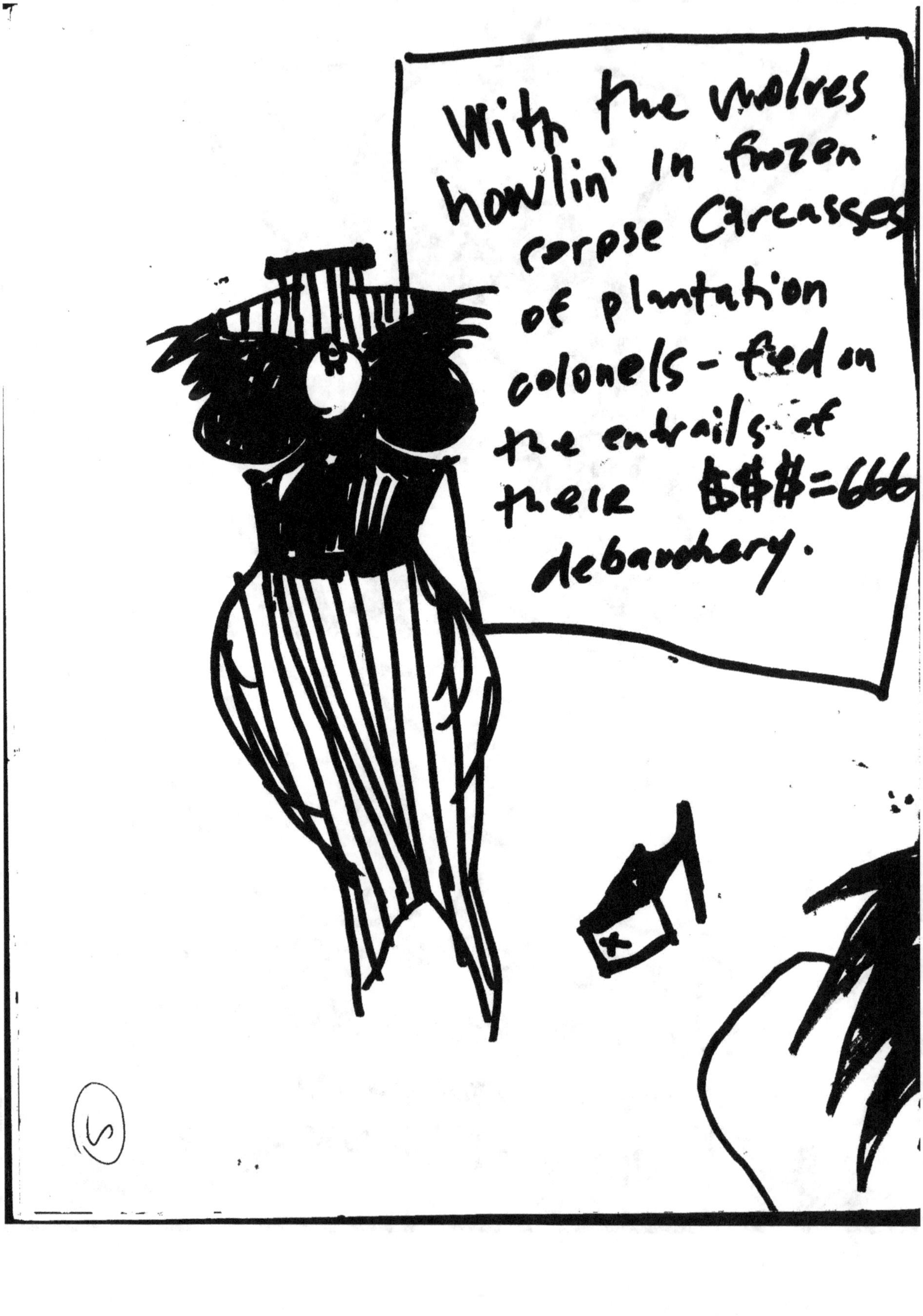
With the wolves howlin' in frozen corpse carcasses of plantation colonels- fed on the entrails of their $$$=666 debauchery.

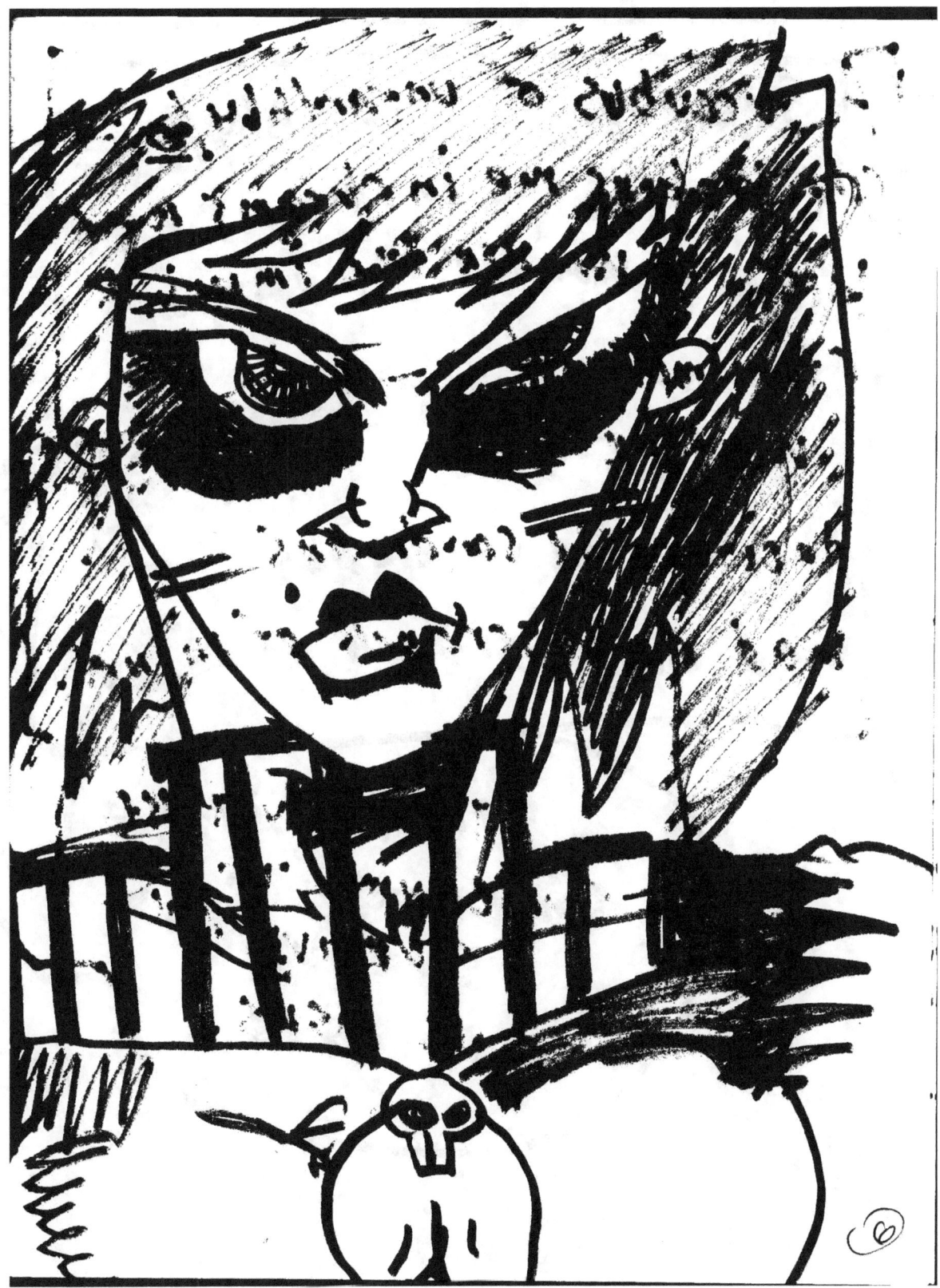

A Succubus of unearthly love
She beckons me in dreams wet
kiss - to wonder the imprint
of mind and
   matter → to
decifer the sandmans
mad dark scrawls of mind.

"THEIR MUST BE
SOME WAY - TO
   SURVIVE?"
SHE ASKS.

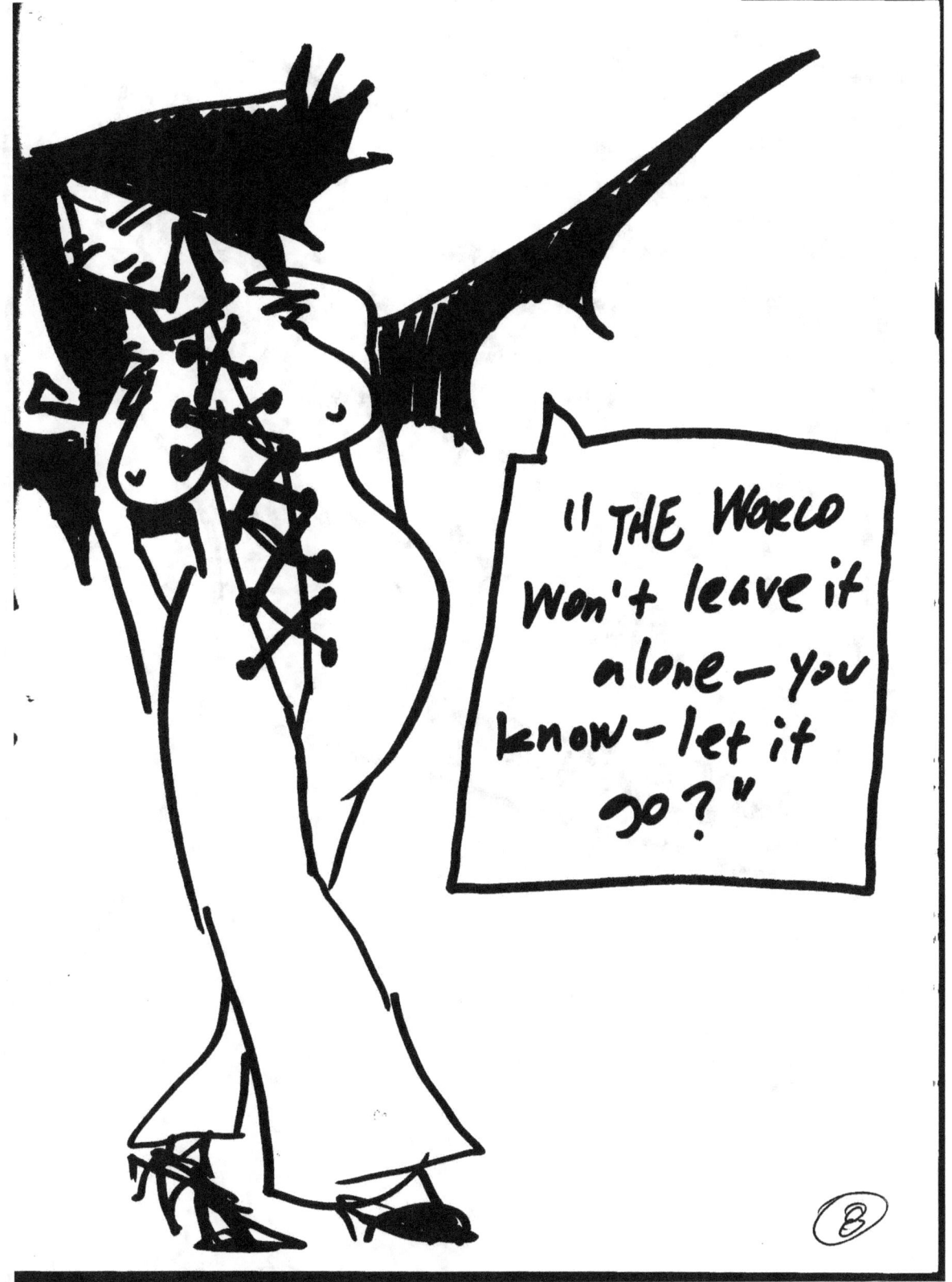

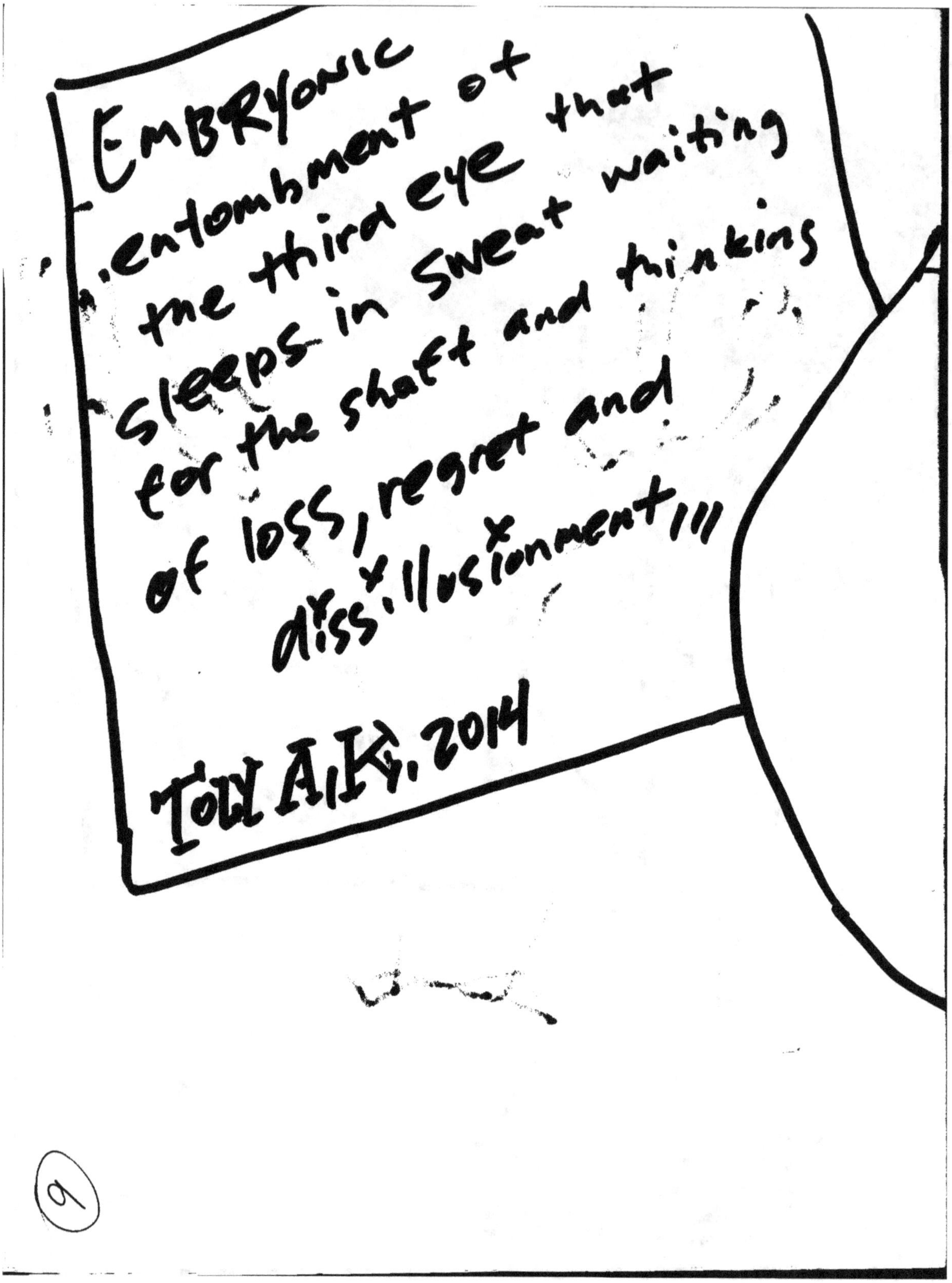
EMBRYONIC entombment of the third eye that sleeps in sweat waiting for the shaft and thinking of loss, regret and dissillusionment!!!
TONY A.K. 2014

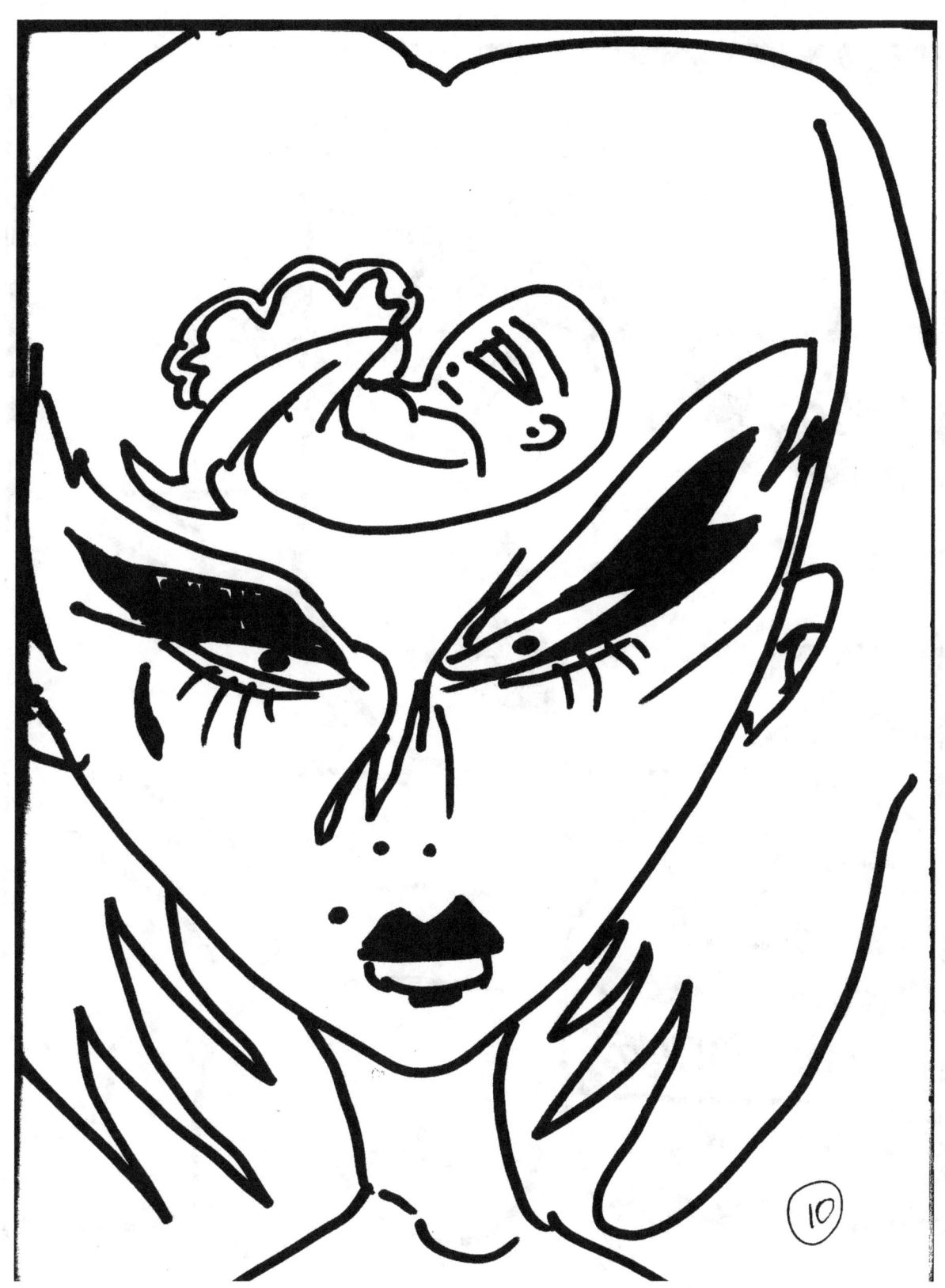

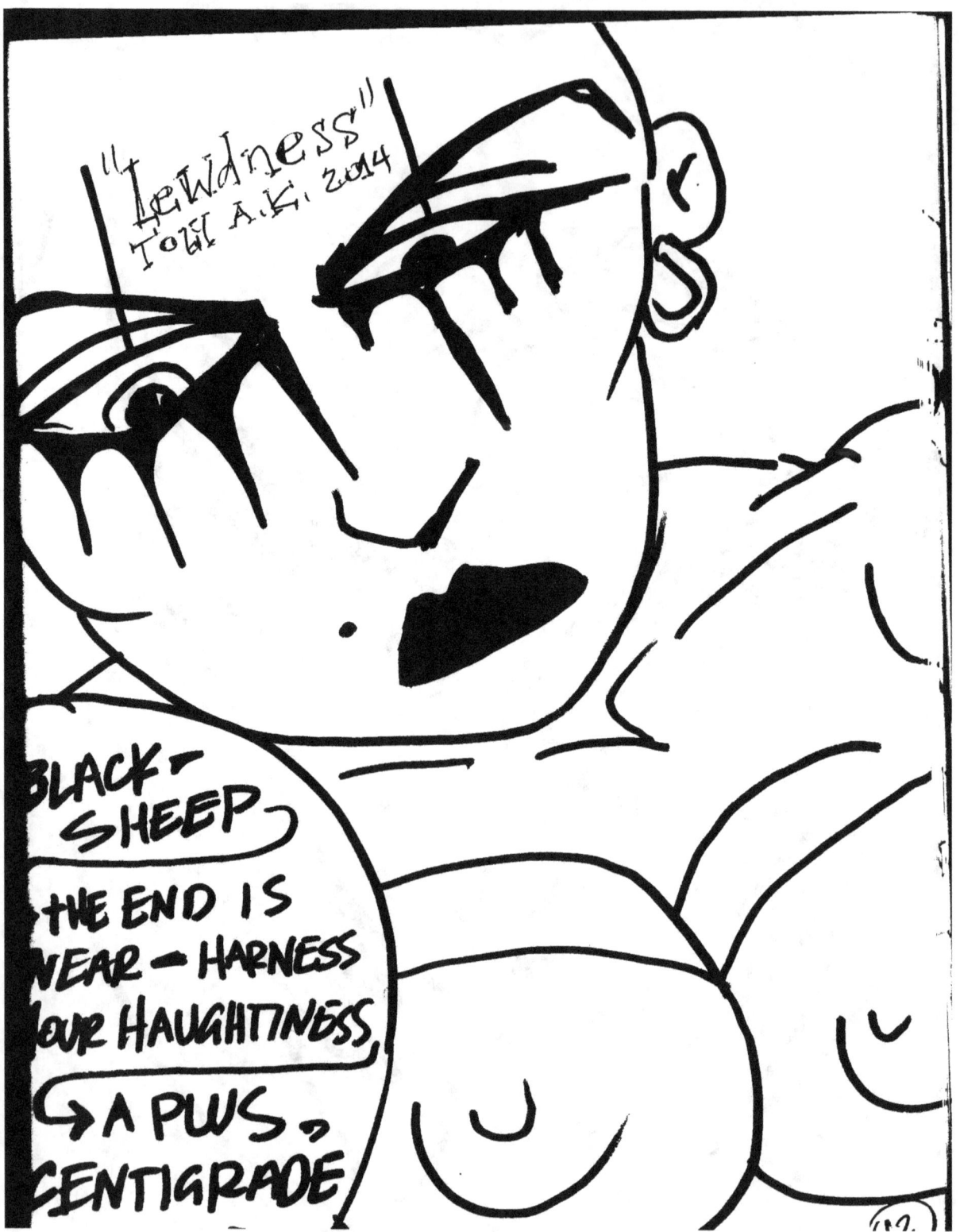

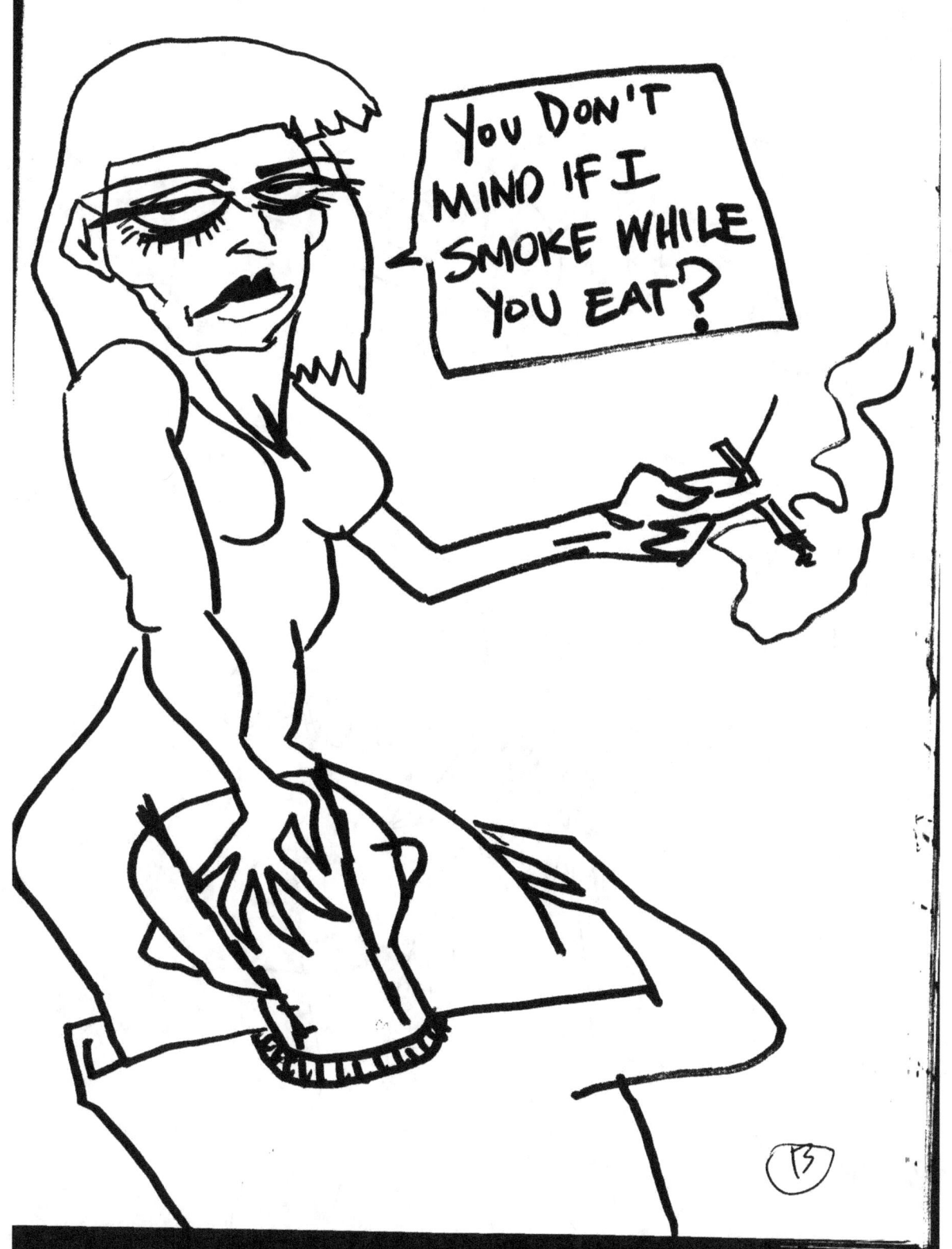

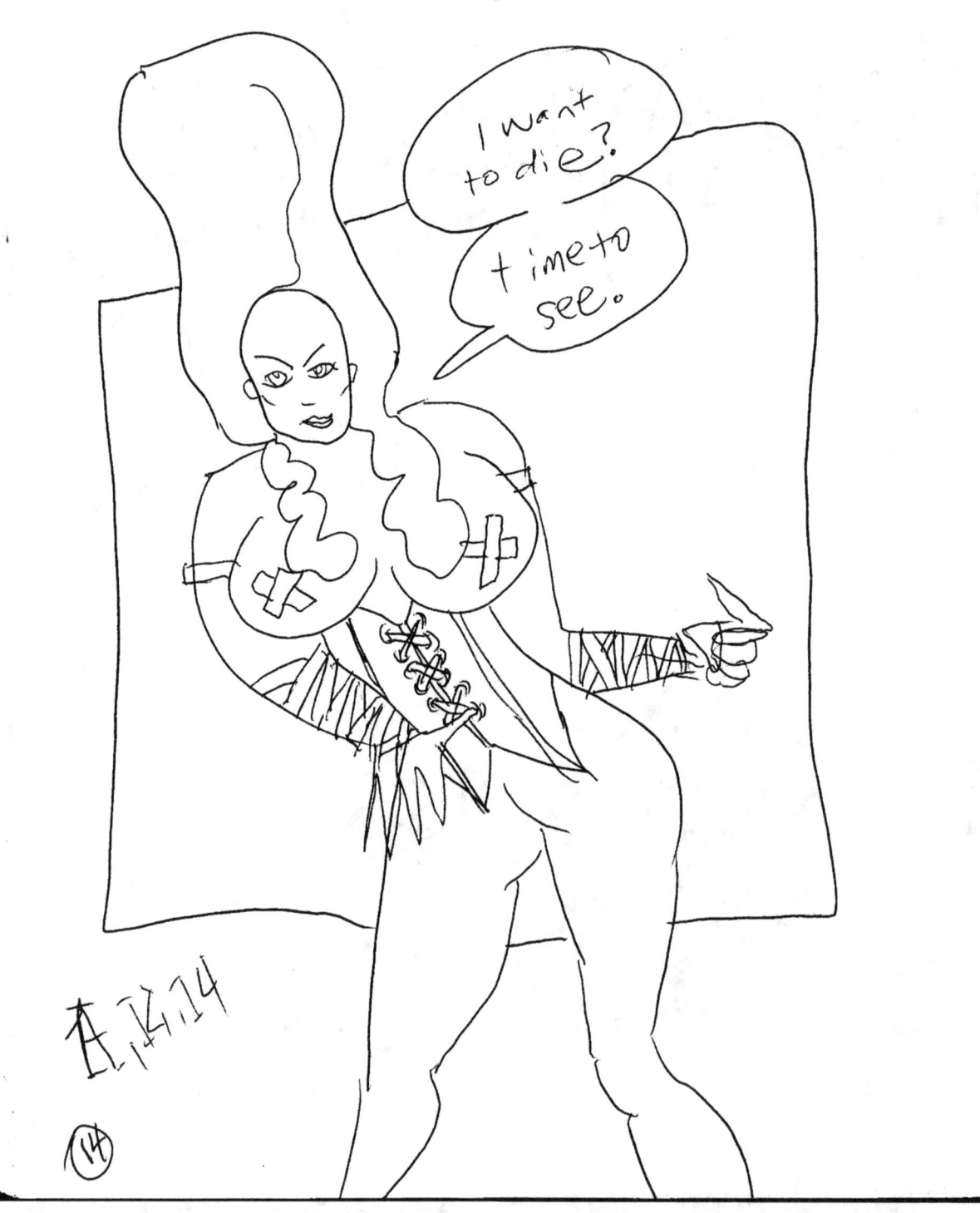

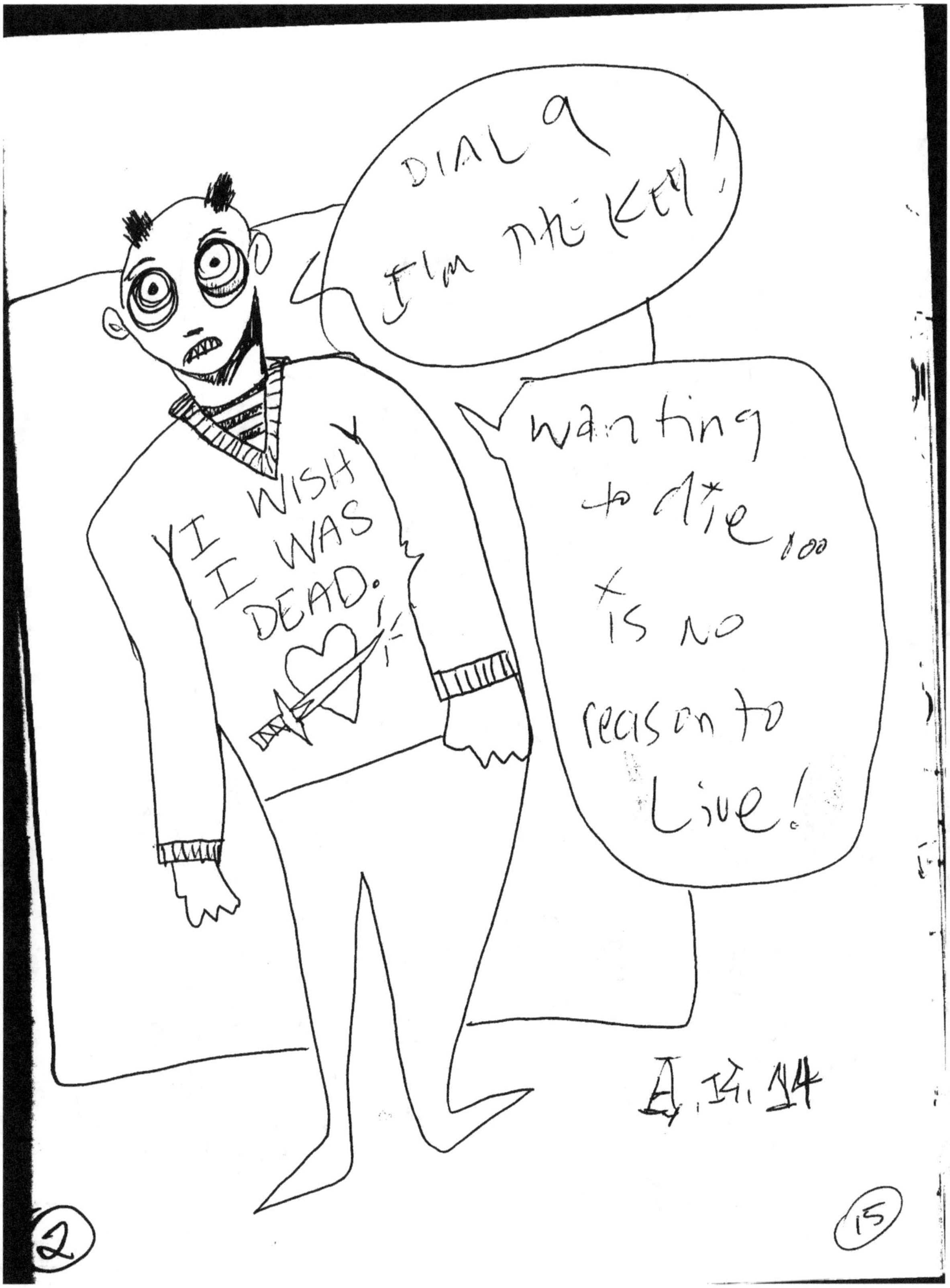
DIAL 9
I'm The Key!
I WISH I WAS DEAD.
wanting to die too is no reason to Live!
2
15

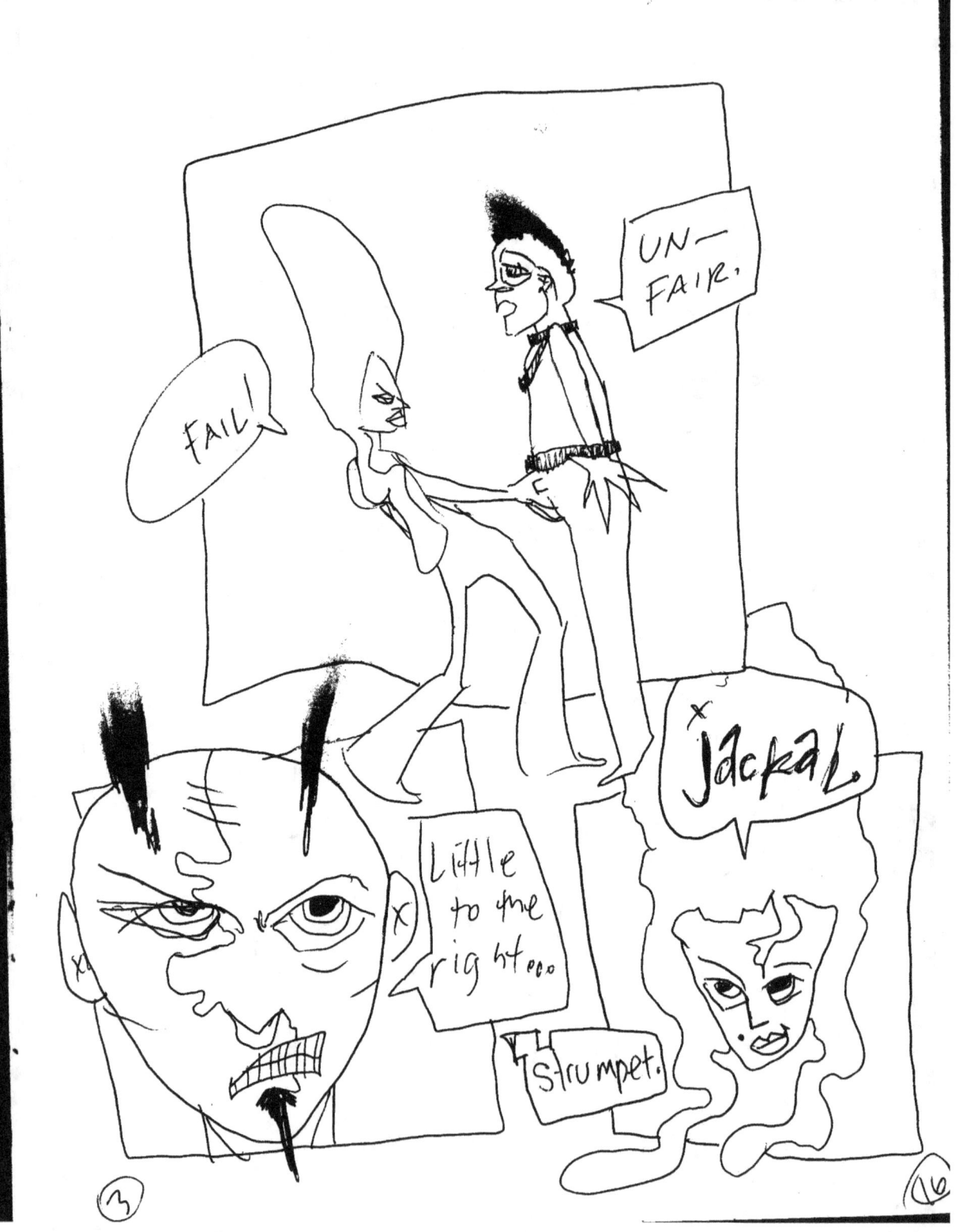

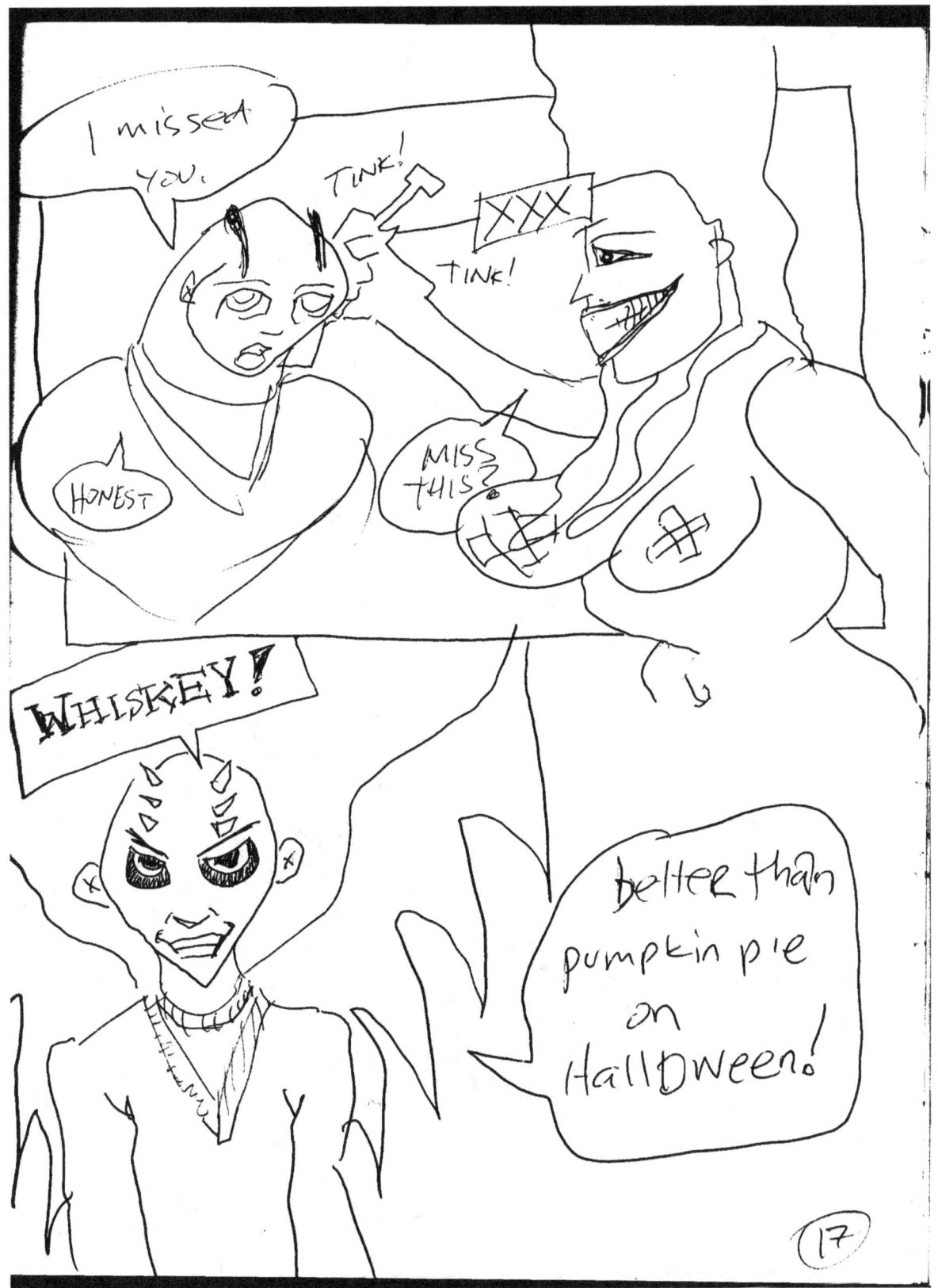

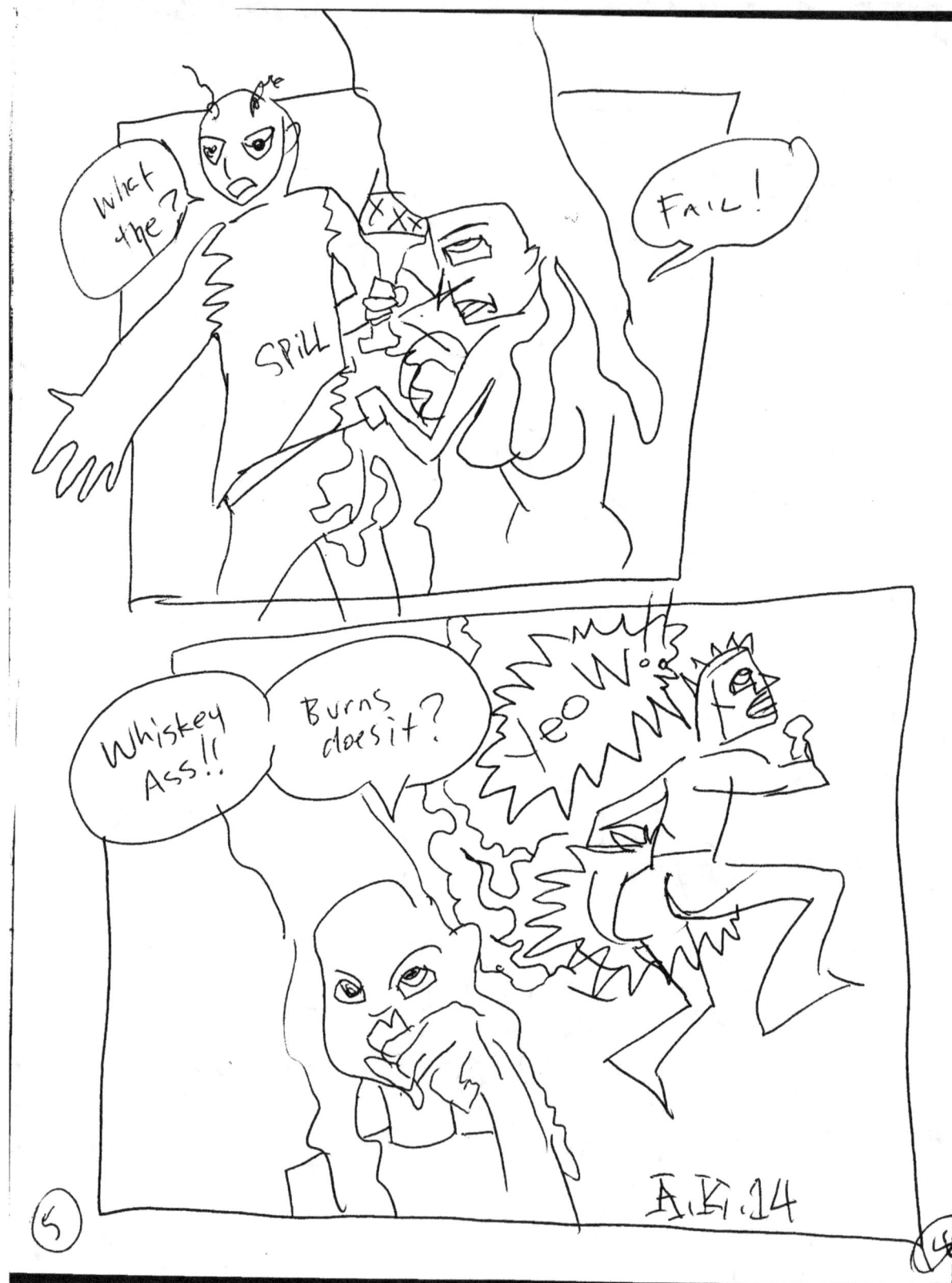

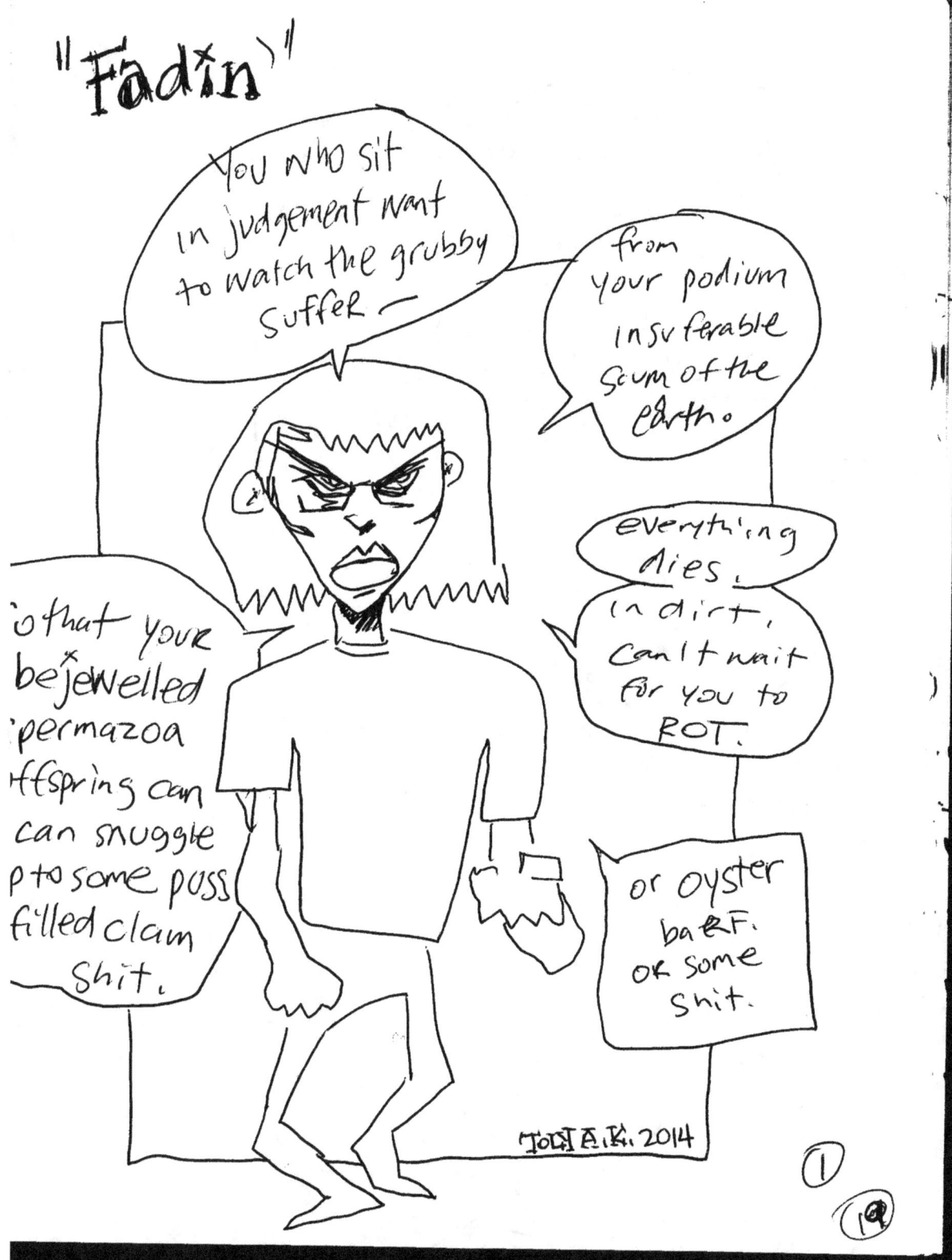

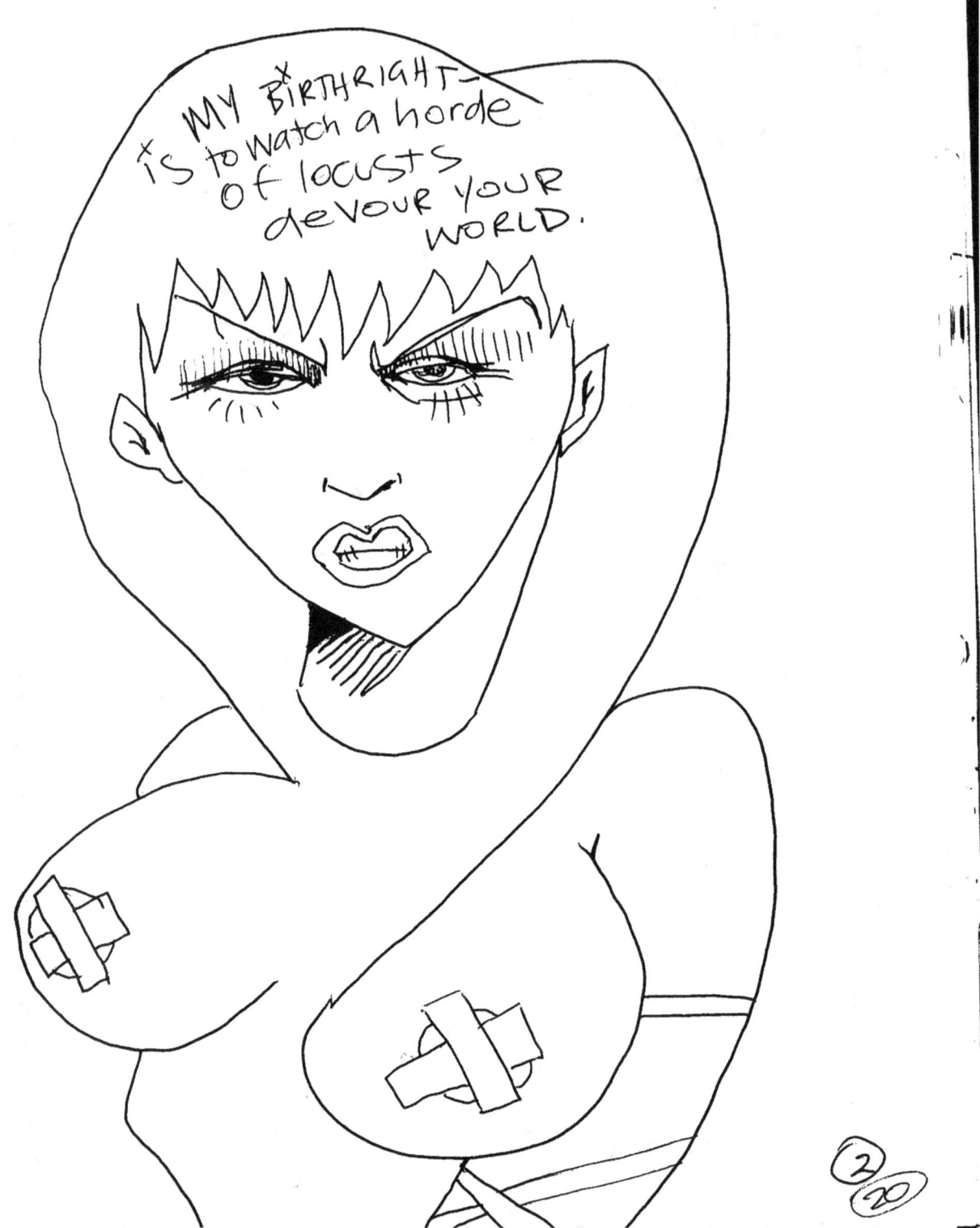

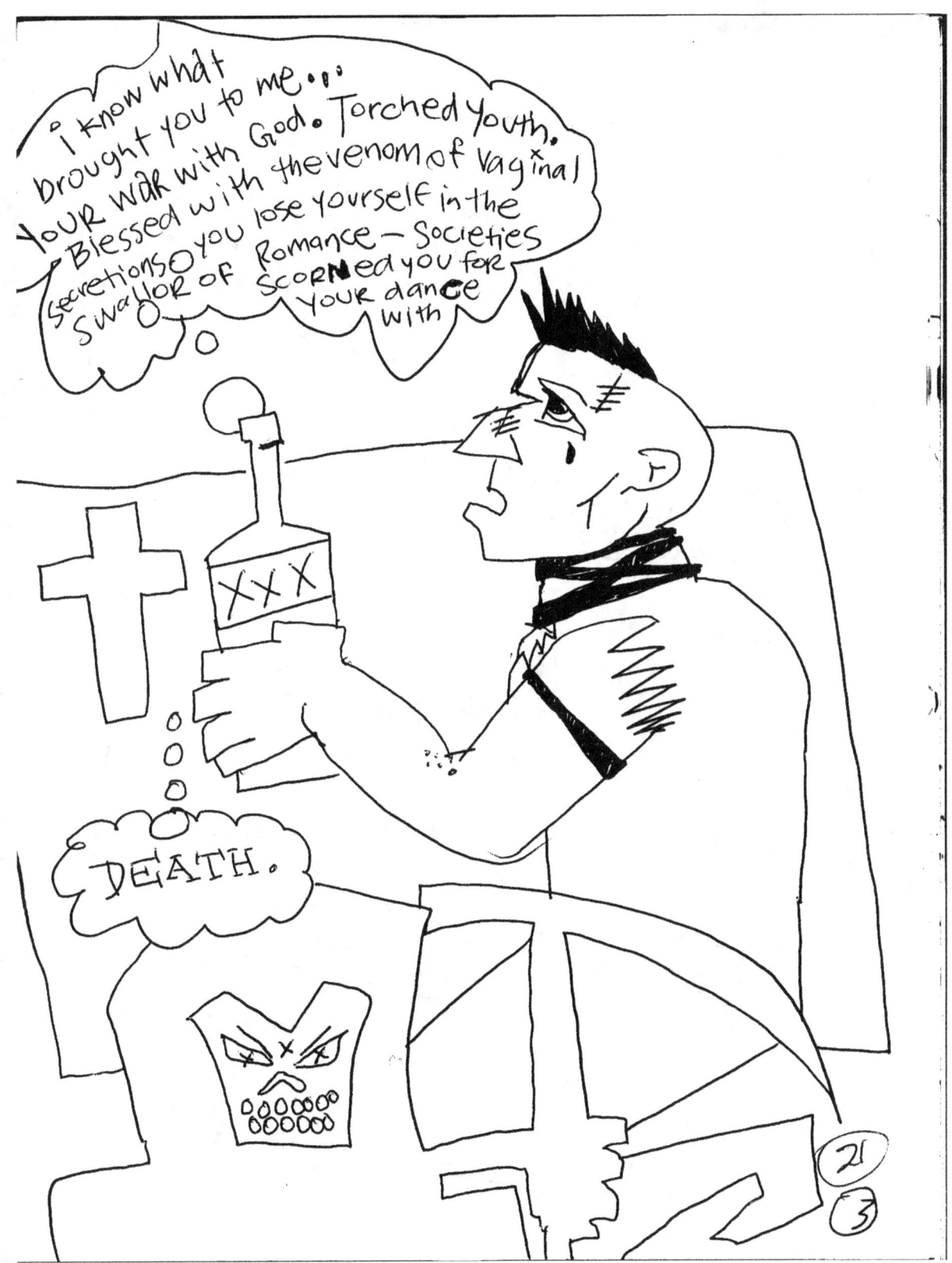

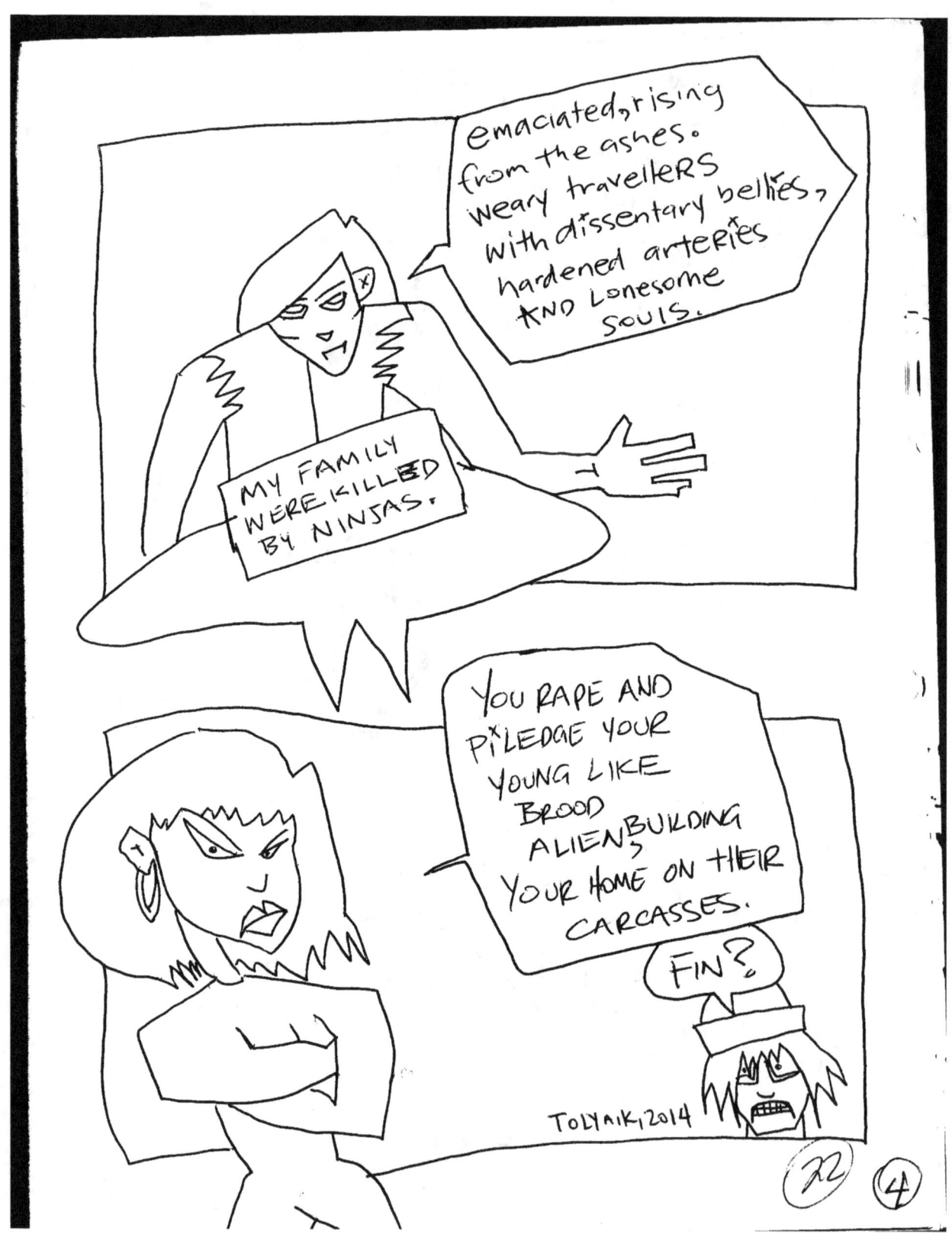

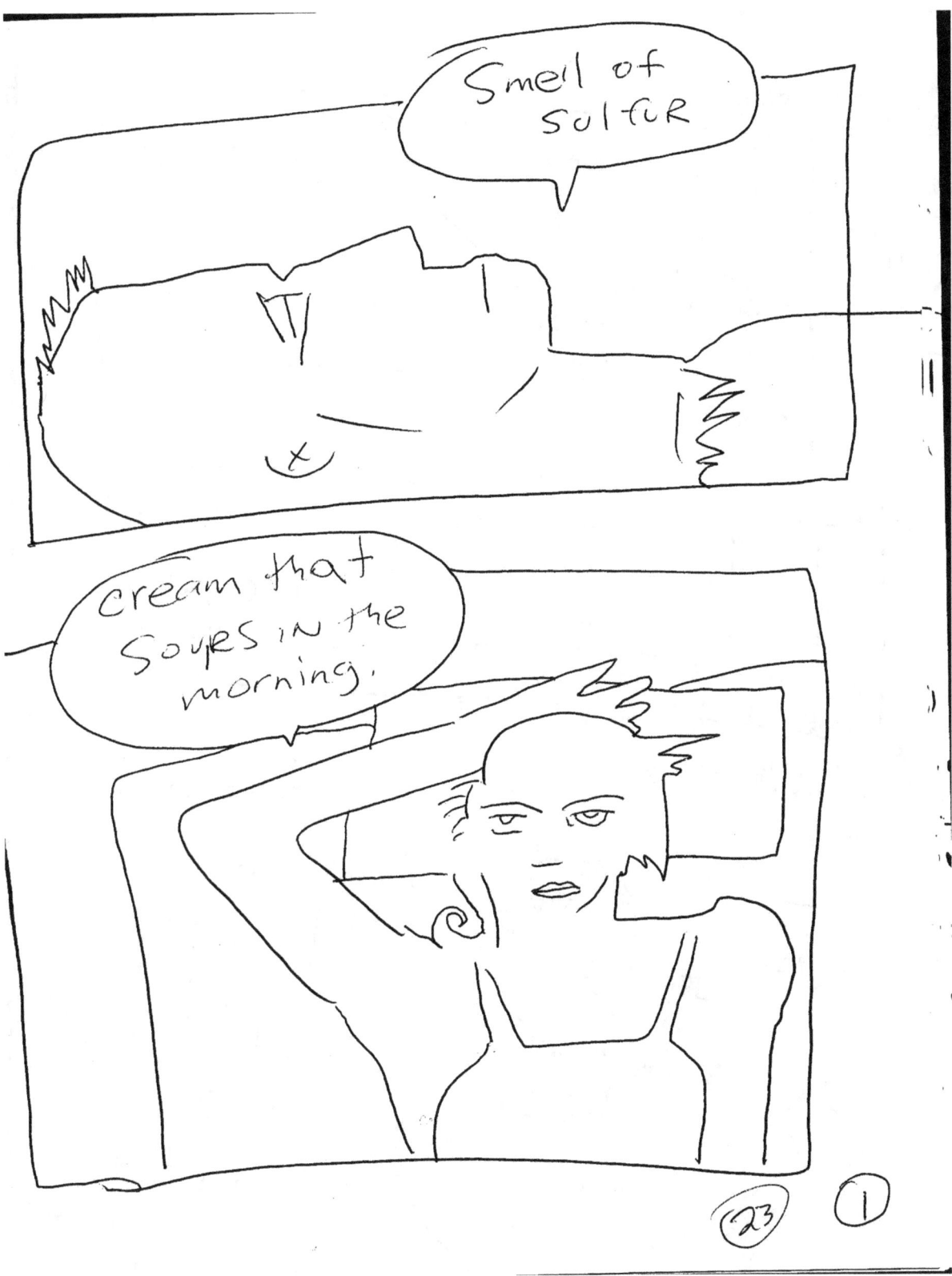

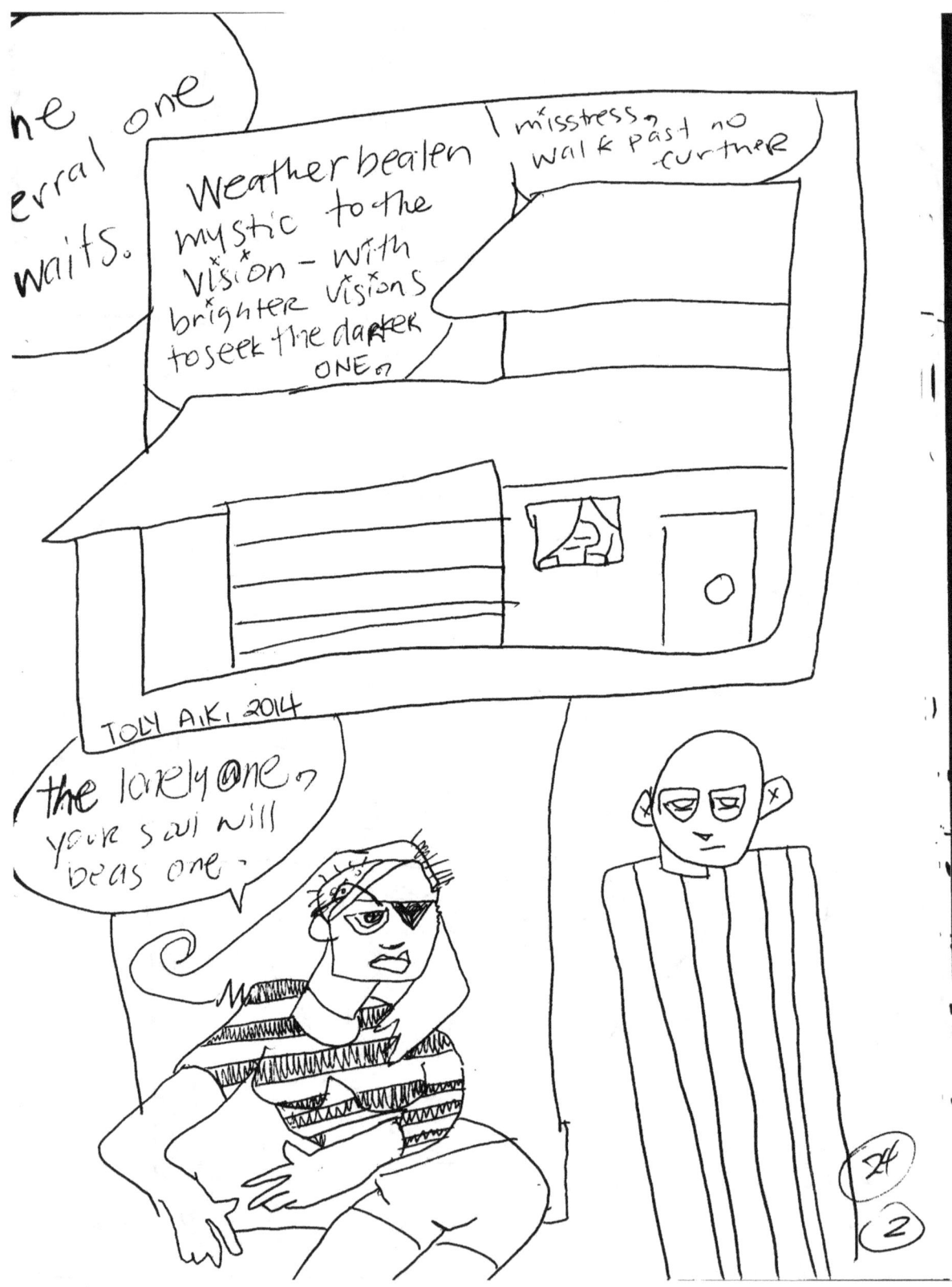

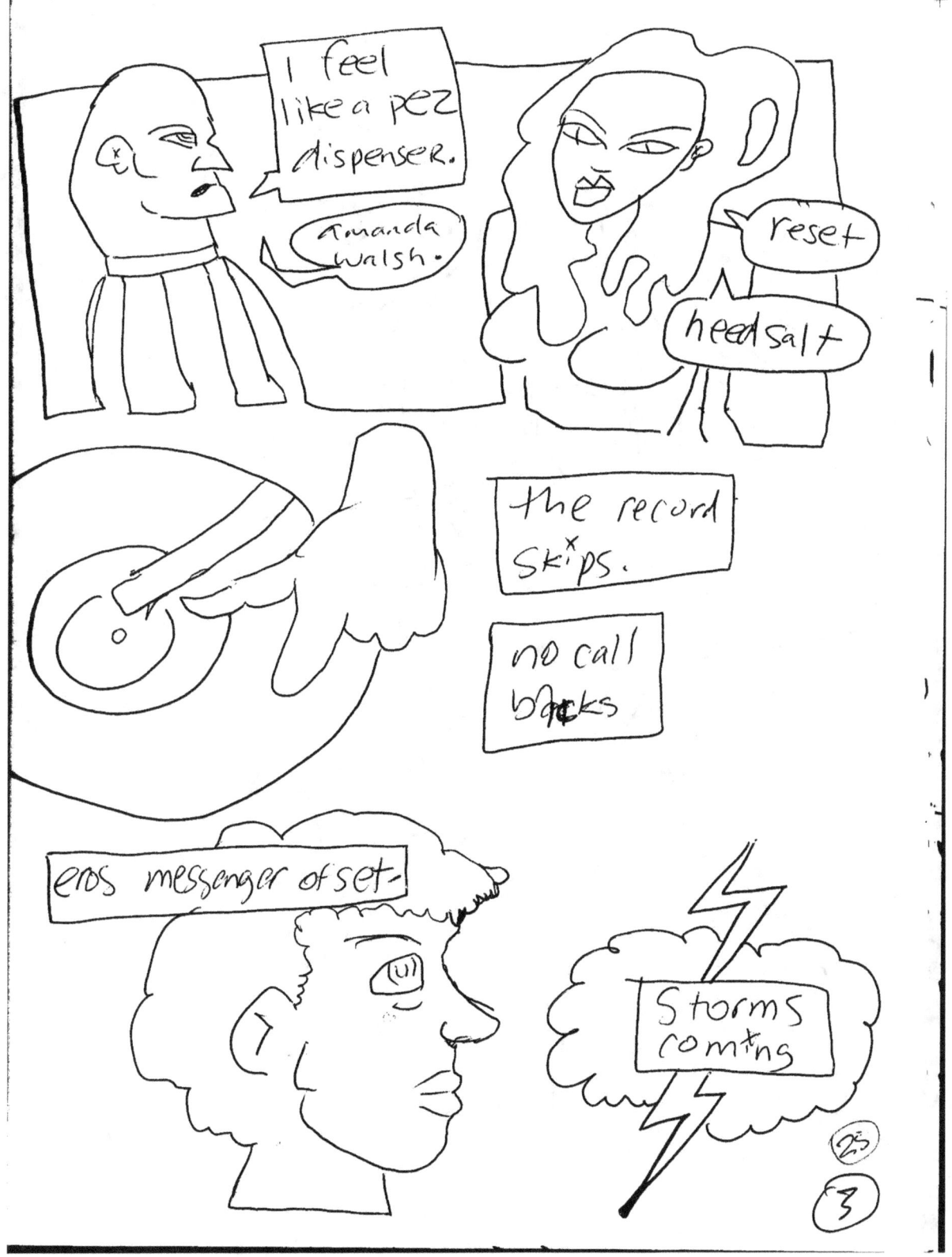

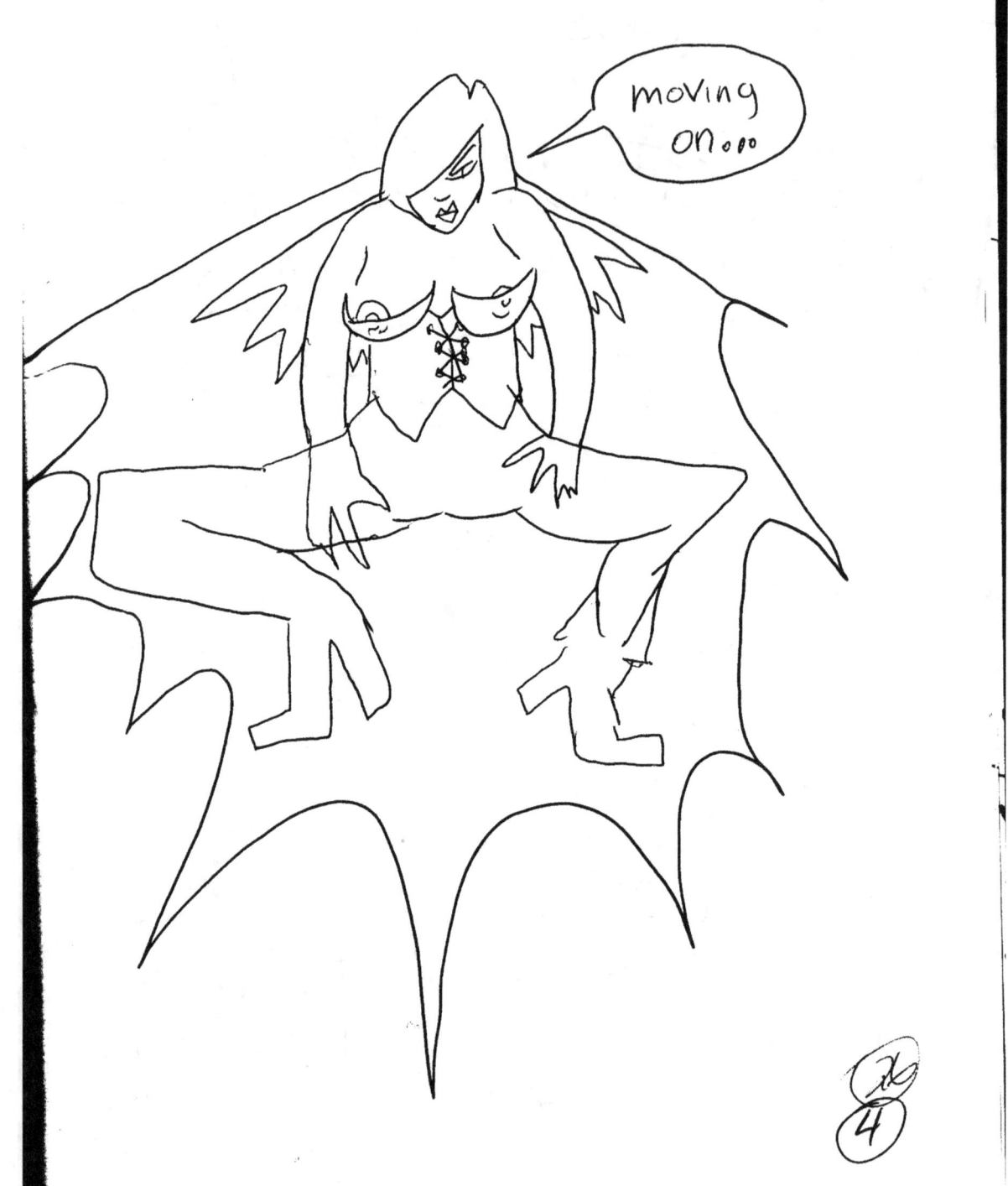

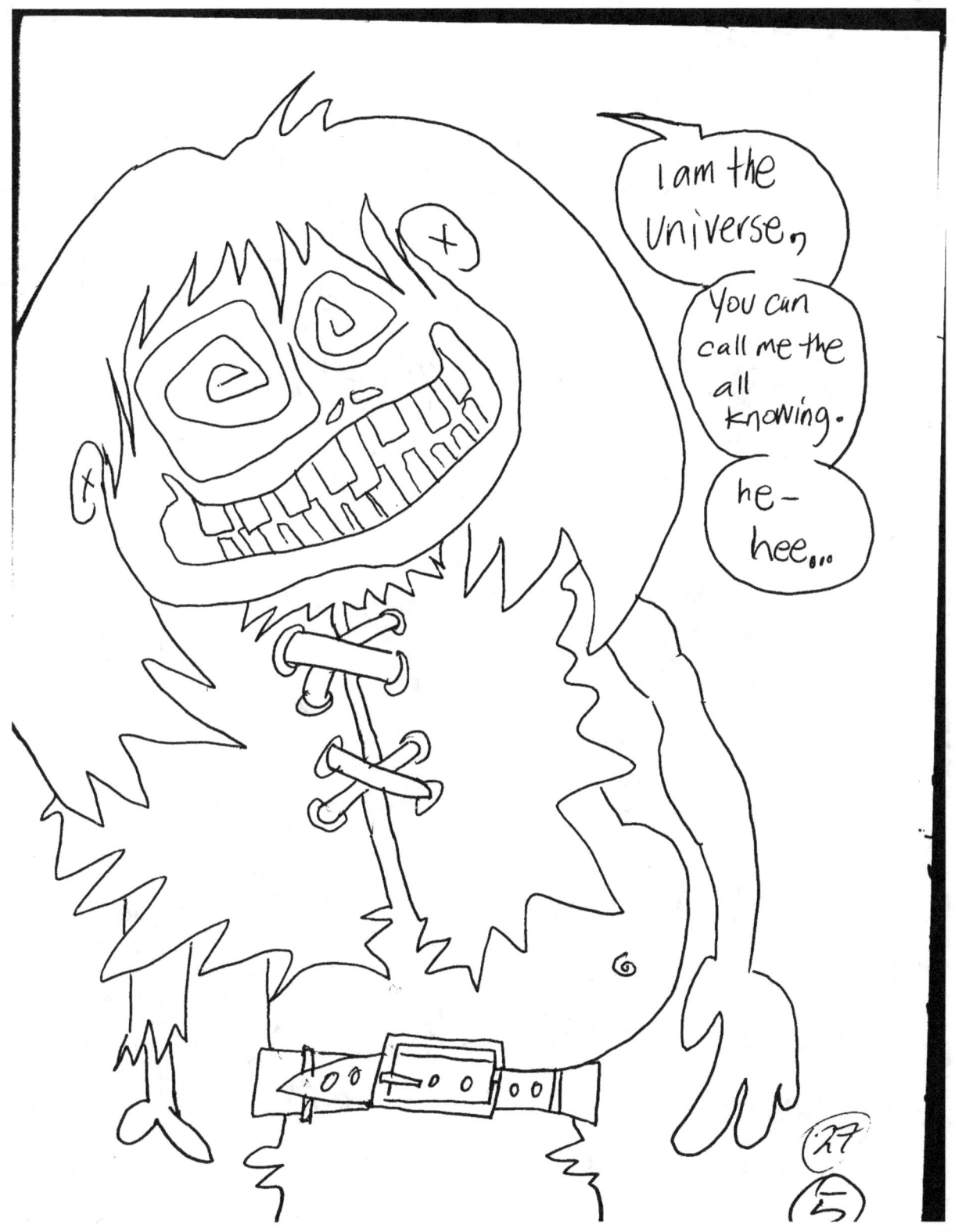

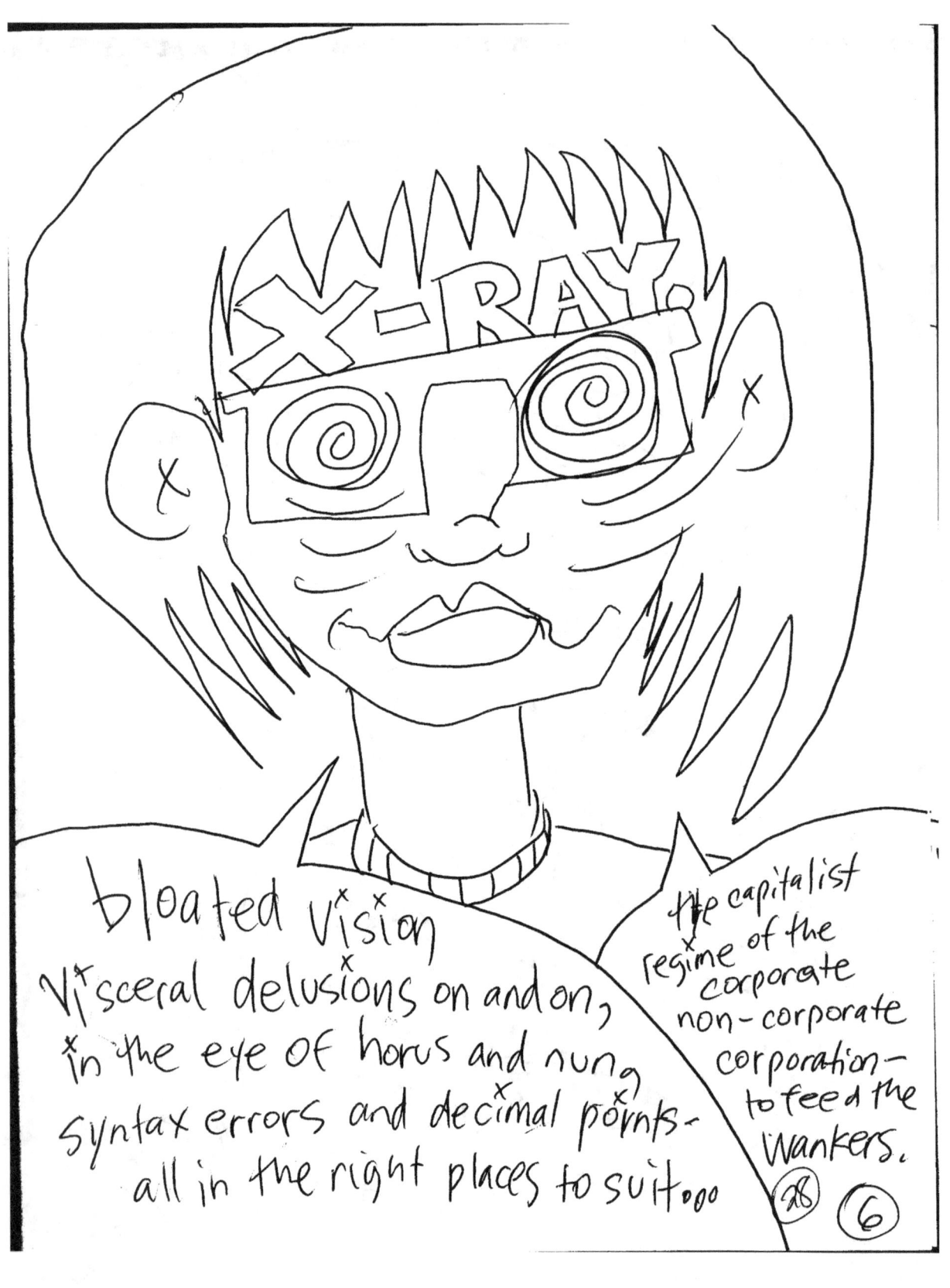